Hark Back to HERSHAM

J.L. & D.M. BARKER

This book is dedicated to the memory of George Greenwood, 6th Nov. 1912-27th Aug. 1985, in recognition of his extensive and invaluable work on the history of Hersham.

INTRODUCTION

Hersham is a village which offers enormous diversity to the historian. Its history is one of contrasts between rich and poor and between the industry and agriculture which have long existed there side by side. The village was dominated in the 19th century by a number of large houses occupied by wealthy families, while at the other end of the scale many of the inhabitants were amongst the poorest in the parish of Walton-on-Thames, of which Hersham formed a part until 1851. Walton was a large parish with a scattered population, of whom, according to the 1851 census, about half were either occupied in agriculture or related work or were employed in domestic service. Hersham was an isolated outpost of the parish, where these tendencies were perhaps most pronounced and which always tended to be the last place to receive new services or facilities: gas street lighting, for example, was not installed here until 1896, although introduced in Walton soon after the formation in 1869 of the Walton & Weybridge Gas Company.

In the 20th century, large houses which came up for sale increasingly tended to be bought by developers, many of the new houses on the estates being sold to commuters. The arrival of the Hackbridge Electrical Construction Company in 1923 initiated an influx of workers who were perceived as competing with local people for the Council houses then under construction.

Although a large part of it lies within the parish of Hersham, I have not covered St. George's Hill in this volume because it was included in our earlier book on Weybridge.

For those interested in the history of Hersham, the late George Greenwood's book "Hersham in Surrey", published in 1986, is highly recommended and is still available from Elmbridge Museum.

Both Elmbridge Museum and the Walton and Weybridge Local History Society have assisted greatly in the preparation of this book and, as with my earlier work, "A Window on Walton-on-Thames", I have found the memories of local people, whether conveyed to me in person, published by the Society or preserved in the Museum's files, a valuable source of material. I have also benefited again from the generosity of one of the country's foremost postcard dealers as well as that of the many local people who have made precious family photographs available.

As in all our books, I have attempted to follow a topographical arrangement, which I hope will prove easy to follow.

JOCELYN BARKER
November 1996

FRONT COVER: Hersham Green c.1912, c.1935 and 1996.

THE METROPOLITAN CONVALESCENT INSTITUTION c.1920 & c.1910

The Metropolitan Convalescent Institution was built in 1854 to provide 300 beds for "the convalescent and debilitated poor" of London, on land given in 1840 by Lord Ellesmere, owner of the St. George's Hill estate. A guide book of 1883 comments: "The salubrity of the spot has been long known to medical men," in contrast to the patients' "own unhealthy and ill-provided homes". The building was designed by J. Clarke and was enlarged in 1862 and 1868. When Oatlands parish was formed in 1869, the siting of St. Mary's Church was influenced by the need to cater for the hospital's patients and, in return, the Hospital contributed funds towards the building of the church. The Convalescent Institution and a small area around it was transferred to the new parish. Miss Connolly, writing in 1966 about her childhood around 1900, recalled that: "During the summer white groups of pathetically sick-looking men and women used to straggle about availing themselves of the many seats provided for them by the wayside." The building later became an N.H.S. geriatric hospital known as the Ellesmere Hospital, which closed in 1989.

WALTON CENTRAL SCHOOL 1929-30

Situated in Mayfield Road, the pioneering Walton Central School was opened by the newly created Surrey Education Committee in 1915 to provide a full-time general education for boys and girls aged 11-15 years. The work included subjects designed to enable them to take up commercial or industrial jobs without further training. The idea was to be copied elsewhere and, by the 1920s, visits from the head teachers of newly-opened central schools were not uncommon. New subjects, such as French and shorthand, and facilities, including a Science Laboratory, were added during the school's early years. It may be noted that, although the school was co-educational, the boys and girls were seated separately.

Pictured here in the front row are: Edna Brown, Anne Peet, Joan Alexander, Dickie Dorman, ?, and Bernard Weedon.

WALTON SECONDARY GIRLS' SCHOOL 1954

In 1938 the boys were transferred to the new school in Ambleside Avenue (now a Middle School) and this building became the Walton Secondary Girls' School. It was demolished in the 1980s. This photograph, taken outside the temporary classrooms backing onto the railway embankment in the background, shows the Upper 5th in July 1954. Pictured are:

Top: Barbara Benge, Marion New, ?, Kathleen Drane, Marie Heudebourck, Susan Eastgate, Carol Davis, Miss Greenfield (form mistress), Patsy Heath, Susan Purkiss, ?, ?, Ann Gibbs, ?, Pamela Willcocks, Margaret Childs.

Centre: Brenda ?, Heather James, Shirley Cross, Mary Cole, Pamela Tummon, Mary Macfarlane, Joan ?, Joan Cross.

Bottom: Janet Lock, Monica Williams, Ann Trodd, Rosemary Cole, Anita Plumbridge, Patricia Brady, ?, Donaly Boxall, Frances Brown, Pauline Stacey.

BURWOOD PARK ESTATE 1927

The name "Burwood", meaning "wood by the fort" - probably a reference to St. George's Hill - was in use by the year 962, but the first gentleman's residence there appears to be that built by John Latton in 1720-21 and insured for £1,000. This seems to be the house which survives, with extensive alterations and additions, as the Burwood Park School. A local guidebook of c.1910 mentions the "extensive conservatories and plantations, and...the orangery, wherein the yellow fruit is successfully cultivated." The last private owner of the house, Miss Frances Askew, died in 1926 and the estate was bought the following year by a property company, who planned to develop the land for housing whilst retaining a park-like character. This aerial view was printed as a postcard with an advertisement on the back for building sites, stressing the good soil, nearby golf courses and other sports centres, and convenient train service to London. An excellent history of Burwood Park by Michael Blackman, recently published by the Walton and Weybridge Local History Society, is available from local bookshops.

THE GREYWOOD CENTRAL RAILWAY, May 1964

In 1946 John Samuel, an engineering entrepreneur, constructed the first section of this railway in the garden of his house, "Greywood", which occupied almost 1 acre of land on the Burwood Park Estate. At this stage there was just under 100 yards of track along the garden's western boundary, passing through a tunnel to a two-road terminus in the front garden. By 1960 a complex layout had evolved, incorporating four stations, several bridges and a viaduct. Except for passing loops at Mount Hoyt and Jacksonville stations the line was single track throughout, and controlled by semaphore signalling with the exception of a small colour-light system at Greywood North. After John Samuel's death on 23rd October, 1962, the railway's future was in doubt until it was purchased late in 1964 by Ian Allan and moved to Hardwick Lane, Lyne. The story of the railway and its subsequent history as the Great Cockrow Railway is contained in a recently-published book by Jeremy Clarke.

BURWOOD PARK ROAD c.1910

The arrival of the railway in 1838 stimulated building development in the area, especially in the vicinity of the railway itself. Burwood Park Road, near the eastern edge of the Poor's Allotments to the south of the railway, did not exist when the Ordnance Survey map of 1867 was drawn up, while Mayfield Road and the southern half of West Grove were marked as Station Road South. Burwood Park Road had four residents listed in Kelly's Directory of 1887. Eleven houses are shown on the map of 1896, including Ascot Lodge, shown here in the left foreground. When this view from the northern end of the road was taken around 1910, Ascot Lodge had already had at least three occupiers, Alfred Pettitt being the latest arrival. By 1916 it was one of five of the 27 houses in the road which were listed as vacant by the Rev. E.P. Pelloe - perhaps one of the consequences of the First World War.

WEST GROVE LOOKING NORTH c.1930

Seen from near the corner of Queen's Road are some of the later houses in West Grove, some built not long before the photograph was taken. In 1937, a planning application was submitted to convert a house called Hayes Leigh near the bend in the background of the photograph into an ice-rink or, alternatively, flats. In a lively discussion in the Council Chamber, the proposal was warmly supported by Mrs. Pennefather, who lived in The White House, opposite the intended site. Mrs. Pennefather argued that there could be no more objection to an ice-rink than to a tennis court, but the application was turned down on the grounds that it would be noisy and that the Council did not wish to set a precedent for allowing a business in a residential district.

WEST GROVE c.1915

West Grove was once known as South Western Grove after the railway company. The map of 1867 shows only four or five houses here. Development began with a few large villas, followed by these humbler dwellings at the northern end of the road nearest the railway. This terrace of late-nineteenth-century villas was known as West Grove Villas. The iron railings in front were, like so many others, removed for the War effort during 1939-45. One of the principal buildings was the White House, built around the 1830s. It stood in extensive grounds, on parts of which Woodside and Charlton Avenues were later built. Former residents of West Grove include Sir William Heaton Horrocks of Birchmead, knighted for his work on malaria, his son Brian, a future General, and Julie Andrews, whose parents lived at Old Meuse.

MAIL COACH 1911

The last horse-drawn mail coach used in the district is shown here in West Grove in 1911, with the Royal cypher of George V recently painted on its sides. It is driven by George Frederick Reed and pulled by a horse named Roger. The coach travelled between Shepperton, Walton and Hersham. The main post office, formerly situated in Church Street, Walton, was replaced in 1908 by the present building in Hersham Road, a little north of the Halfway. Several postal deliveries per day were the normal practice at this time and it is recorded that, in the 1890s, the postmen in the Walton area made three delivery rounds on Sundays! Letter boxes were emptied with corresponding frequency and it was still possible at the time of this photograph to send a postcard in the morning in the knowledge that it would reach its destination by tea-time. Roger, no doubt, had plenty of exercise and knew the district intimately!

HALFWAY RAILWAY BRIDGE c.1920

The London & Southampton Railway was opened from Nine Elms to Woking Common on 21st May, 1838. This photograph, taken from the Hersham side, shows the railway bridge at the Halfway. It has always presented a hazard to high vehicles, which would occasionally get stuck under it. Abnormal loads such as the larger Hackbridge transformers were particularly at risk and alternative routes had to be found. In the case of large transformers on low loaders, the Albany Bridge had also to be avoided for fear of grounding. The almshouses can be glimpsed through the trees on the left, while on the right is Ellis & Co.'s wine store where, according to the "Surrey Herald" of December 1937, there was always a "rhyme for the times". The article reported that "It is the rendezvous where the best of wines, spirits and beers are supplied to grace the Christmas festivities."

PLOUGHING AT BELL FARM c.1914

Created when the railway bisected the land in this area in the 1830s, Bell Farm derived its name from T. & G. Bell, who owned it by 1877, when they sold some fields south of Hersham Road to William Alderson. Alderson lived with his family and four servants in a house called Melrose, and he or his mother, Mrs. Jane Elizabeth Alderson, progressively acquired other land in the vicinity to create a large market garden. Mrs. Alderson was listed in the Rate Book as the owner of both Melrose and Bell Farm in 1914 and is named as the market gardener in 1918, which probably explains how her son and his family were able to continue living at Melrose after his bankruptcy in 1911. The market garden was sold to Frederick A. Secret some time before 1924. Rydens School and Bell Farm Middle School were both built on the Bell Farm land, opening in 1952 and 1958 respectively.

HERSHAM ROAD c.1920

This view, taken from the corner of West Grove by the railway bridge, shows on the right the recently-rebuilt almshouses, surrounded by a fence and trees as ordered by the Walton Vestry in 1809. The road had been widened in 1906, many of its flanking trees and hedges being lost in the process, and the fence and smaller trees shown in front of the almshouses are no doubt replacements dating to that time. On the left can be seen some of the shops and houses which were built in this area following the arrival of the railway. Immediately adjacent to the railway bridge, and not shown here, were the 19th-century Railway Cottages, and the later row of shops next to them were known as 1-3, Bridgeborough Buildings, reflecting this proximity. The Radium Laundry occupying the shop in the foreground would have sounded less alarming before the health risks from radiation were understood! The petrol pumps a little further along are a reminder that this was a time of transition from horse-drawn to motor transport.

ALMSHOUSES c.1900

In Hersham Road, just south of the corner of West Grove, stood these almshouses. Their origin is obscure, although a theory was put forward in 1870 that they might have been built with money from Henry Hylton's bequest of 1640, and for this reason they became known from the late 19th century as Hylton's Almshouses. The occupants were nominated by the Vicar and churchwardens from amongst the poor people of the parish of Walton-on-Thames (including, of course, Hersham). They lived here rent-free, but were not necessarily given any pension. The row of eight small cottages with a hipped roof seems to have been built during the second or third quarter of the 18th century, an additional cottage being added, with the Vestry's permission, at the west end in 1802 by Mr. C.B. Renshaw as part of an arrangement with Mary Stent, widow, who was its first occupier.

ALMSHOUSES c.1910

The 18th-century almshouses shown above had deteriorated by the end of the nineteenth century and in 1896 the new Urban District Council expressed their view that they should be rebuilt. The trustees duly replaced them between 1902 and 1912 with these semi-detached alms cottages. Kelly's Directory of 1911 states that at that time there were "six almshouses, erected in 1903 at a cost of £1,200, for poor men and women who have not received parish relief for 5 years." By 1920 the number had increased to nine dwellings, together with a caretaker's lodge. They were in turn replaced in 1966 by the present Mayfield Homes, built with funds from the Walton Charities and consisting of 32 flats, a Warden's residence and communal rooms and garden.

HERSHAM ROAD FROM THE AIR 1926

This oblique view from the south shows the comparatively undeveloped character of Hersham Road in the 1920s. The stretch of road nearest to the railway is moderately built up and Fellcott Road, laid out about 1900 (around the same time as the former Felcott Lane was renamed Hersham Road), by now had houses along parts of both sides. The major part of Hersham Road south of the railway, however, is bordered by fields, most of which had been part of William Alderson's market garden. This had by this time been bought by Frederick A. Secret. The buildings of Bell Farm can be seen at the end of Fellcott Road on the site now occupied by Rydens School.

RYDENS GROVE c.1910

In 1869 Hersham Road - then known as Felcott Lane - boasted few buildings, and neither Rydens Grove nor the streets in the Thistlecroft area to the south of Hersham Road had yet been built. Fields lay on both sides of Hersham Road, although a small group of houses was in existence on the south side near the corner of Molesey Road. By 1896 the whole area had developed considerably and a small hamlet was growing up, although housing development along Rydens Grove and some of the other new streets was still sparse. The grocer's shop and post office on the corner of Rydens Grove at 283 Hersham Road, of which one end is shown here in the left foreground, seems to have been built in the last few years of the nineteenth century and was run until at least 1910 by Mrs. Alice Hall Smith. Nearly 100 years later it is still in business. As the photograph shows, by about 1910 Rydens Grove was a fully developed residential street.

RYDENS GROVE LAUNDRY c.1910

The laundry at Laurel Cottage - now no. 1 Rydens Grove - is believed to have been started in the early 1890s, and in 1904 was run by Charles Pawley. It was bought c.1906 by Mr. Henry C. Scales of Kits Coty in Hersham Road, who is shown here standing in front of the premises with nine employees. In 1916 he was advertising "High-class family work. Moderate charges. Open air drying grounds." The last feature was still stressed in an advertisement of c.1935. Mr. Scales died in 1951 and his son C.C. Scales, who had joined the business in 1930, carried it on until it closed in 1965. He then let the property to a lighting firm and eventually sold it to the present owners in 1986.

A. TENNISWOOD'S CARS c.1922

Mr. A.H.H. Tenniswood seems to have set up business as a blacksmith in Queen's Road, Hersham, about 1906 and continued there for several years. By 1911 he had diversified by going into partnership with Mr. E. Martin of Hersham Road as a fly proprietor. (A fly was the horse-drawn equivalent of the modern taxi.) As a blacksmith, he would have been capable of carrying out his own maintenance work on the vehicles. By 1916 he was living at 1, Osborne Villas, one of the late-19th-century houses at the Molesey Road end of Hersham Road, although it is clear from an advertisement of February 1919 that his business had closed down during the 1914-18 War. In 1920 he was advertising "Taxi Cabs always available; ready day or night for any distance." The photograph shows three of his Renault cars on contract to Burhill Golf Club about 1922. The registration numbers indicate that these vehicles were of pre-First World War vintage, and registered in different places, suggesting that he bought them second-hand after the War.

WALTER BROWN'S COAL CART c.1910

The Brown family came to Hersham in 1890. Walter Brown started a business as a coal dealer and furniture remover at 125 Molesey Road, with an entrance off Rydens Grove. His brother George, who took over the business around 1912-15, is shown here with a cart loaded with coal - the cheaper coal being carried on one side of the cart, with the better quality fuel on the other. The horse's ear muffs served to keep out the coal dust which had to be washed off the animal each night. A price of 2s 10d. (approx. 18p) per hundredweight can be seen on the dividing board. By 1939 George Brown had two motor lorries, one of which was commandeered during the Second World War, while the business continued to operate using the other, which was also available for hire. Each year the lorry would be cleaned up and covered over to transport four families and their belongings to Staplehurst in Kent for the hop-picking.

MINSTREL TROUPE c.1919

One of George Brown's coal carts is shown here, decorated probably in preparation for the Armistice celebrations in 1919. The British and American flags, together with the presence of two sailors in uniform, suggest that occasion, while the young lady in the centre front is wearing the front page of a newspaper (possibly the "Surrey Comet") across her chest. Even the policeman is wearing a rosette on his uniform. Another garment worthy of note is the old farmworker's smock worn by the driver. The blacked-up men were probably an established local minstrel troupe - a popular form of entertainment during the early decades of the 20th century. An unusual feature is the white patch around the right eye of many of the men. Hersham appears to have boasted at least one such group, as the "Surrey Advertiser" in March 1906 reported on a highly successful entertainment given by the Snowball Minstrels in aid of Hersham Young Men's Club.

HERSHAM STATION 1959

In 1928 a large housing estate, to be named the Esher Place Estate, was planned on land between the River Mole and Molesey Road. The Railway Company put aside £19,000 in its estimates for 1929 to build a station there. The intended estate was never built, but the money remained in reserve and was eventually used to build Hersham Station, which opened on Monday, 28th September, 1936. Car parking facilities were advertised at 1s. (5p) per day or 5s. (25p) per week, and 3d. per day or 1s. per week for cycles. In 1937 the Council wrote to the London Passenger Transport Board in support of an application for a bus service along Molesey Road, but the potential number of passengers to Hersham Station was not yet considered sufficient to justify a new or diverted bus service. This photograph was taken from the 11.27 a.m train from Waterloo to Alton on 24th August, 1959, and shows the 11.30 a.m. Waterloo to Bournemouth train, pulled by the Lord Nelson class locomotive no. 30858, "Lord Duncan", overtaking the other train in the station.

F.W. SAUNDERS' TRUCKS c.1925

Walter Saunders, from Ardingley, Sussex, settled in Hersham about 1890 and set up as a contractor from Stag House, 10 Green Lane Avenue. Albert, the eldest of his thirteen children had been born at the Barley Mow on an earlier visit. Another son, F.W. Saunders, started in motorised haulage around 1924 and continued until 1939 when his six vehicles were taken for war service. The photograph shows two Chevrolet lorries in his yard at Molesey Road. His son, Bernard, in turn started in haulage in 1950 with a 1939 petrol engined Leyland Lynx, after completing his National Service.

THE WHEELER'S REST CAFE September 1968

This cafe and shop in Molesey Road adjacent to F.W. Saunders' premises was run by Mr. Buck until taken over by Saunders in 1962. The photograph shows the premises during the flooding which began when heavy rain caused the River Mole to burst its banks on Sunday, 15th September, 1968. At about 4.00 p.m. the flooding reached the Cottimore Lane area of Walton and by 10.30 p.m. the water had spread as far as The Grove. The Council Surveyor's initial estimate of the cost, excluding any charges from the emergency services, was £28,934. A large-scale flood prevention scheme for the Mole Valley was subsequently initiated by the County Council and the Thames Conservancy.

THE OLD HOUSE AT HOME c.1910

Two brewer's draymen are shown here posing for the camera outside the Old House at Home, a beerhouse in operation from at least the 1870s. In 1892 the pub was said to be frequented principally by farm labourers. The man on the right is perhaps the landlord, thought to have been either William Chatfield or George Barnes, both listed as beer retailers here in directories around this time. The old building was popularly known as "The Dust Hole" on account of the dust which blew in under the door in windy weather. It was a popular resort of the gypsies who camped nearby and who liked to race their horses along Molesey Road between here and the horse trough near the Barley Mow.

TUG OF WAR TEAM c.1930

Pictured outside the same door at the Old House at Home are a sturdy winning team of men with their rope. Sadly, their names are not recorded and we have been unable to trace an account of the match in which they had been competing. The man in the centre, behind the beer bottles, is perhaps the pub's landlord, D. Dixie. The pub was rebuilt in the 1930s and when it re-opened Mr. Dixie's son Jack took over the licence. In March 1939, the new premises being in operation, the Old House at Home was granted a full licence for the first time.

BELL FARM RECREATION GROUND, 30th May, 1953

Hersham's first recreation ground, near the Barley Mow, was bought by the Council in 1923, but replaced by another behind Mole Road in 1938 in anticipation of its destruction by the building of the Hersham Bypass. In 1950-51, half of the new Recreation Ground was given up for Council housing, and the Coronation Fields were purchased in its place and named the Bell Farm Recreation Ground. On 29th May, 1953, three days before the Coronation, Hersham Robins Cycle Speedway Club, hitherto handicapped by the lack of their own ground, opened their new track there. This had been laid out by the Council at no cost to the club. Councillor W.L. Sims initiated the proceedings by robing Hersham's Coronation Maid of Honour, 19-year-old Miss Ivy Bleault, after which Miss K. Monahan, the new Chairman of the Council, performed the opening ceremony. She was presented with a bouquet by Bill Head, the Robins' Captain. The afternoon's speedway events included a challenge match between the Robins and Chiswick Comets which the Robins narrowly lost by three points. There was also a children's fancy dress competition. The occasion was blessed with better weather than Coronation Day itself, which proved to be cold and wet, so that the celebrations were pronounced "disappointing" by the "Surrey Herald". Despite being used for both these events, the Recreation Ground itself was not officially opened until later in the year.

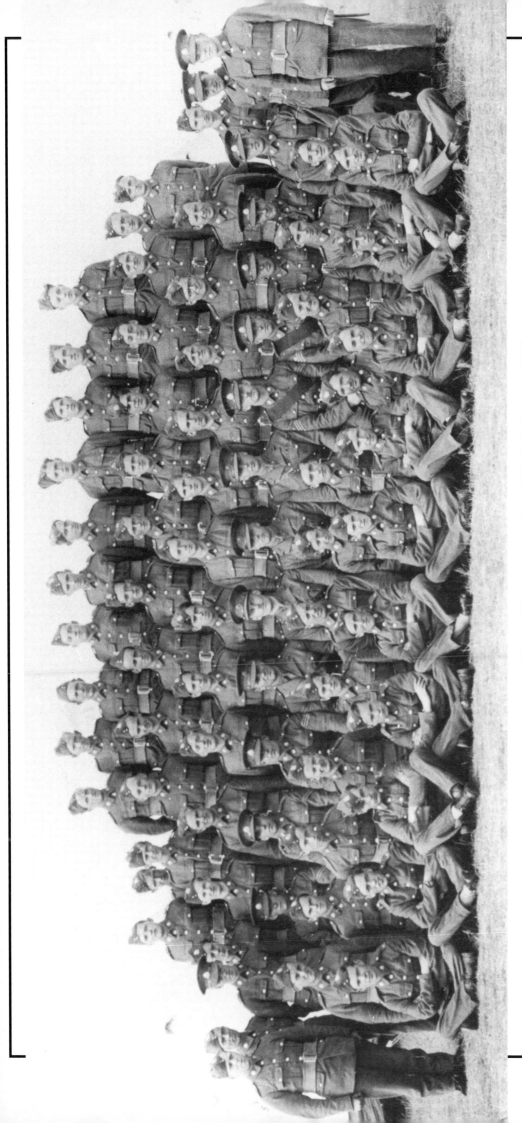

"A" COMPANY, 1/6th EAST SURREY REGIMENT, July-August 1939

The 19th-century Volunteer Battalions were reorganised into the Territorial Force in 1908 and the 3rd Volunteer Battalion became the 6th East Surrey Regiment. The Regiment was permitted to retain its full-dress "rifle" uniform and rifle drill until 1927. In September 1913 the new Territorial Drill Hall was opened in Molesey Road in an effort to boost recruitment. The Esher and District Detachment of the 6th East Surrey Regiment's Headquarters was transferred there. The Territorial Force was renamed the Territorial Army in 1920. By summer 1938, the Battalion was over 1,200 strong, and whilst at the annual training camp in Lympne, Kent, 30th July-13th August, 1939, they were split into two: the Kingston and Hersham detachments and the Band becoming the 1/6th Battalion, whilst the remainder became the 2/6th Battalion. This photograph, taken at the camp, shows the Hersham detachment.

MOLESEY ROAD c.1930

From just south of the corner of Rydens Grove, the view northwards along Molesey Road in 1930 was not very different from its modern appearance. The shortage of low-cost housing after the First World War had resulted in the Government's laying on local authorities the duty of providing such homes. In 1926 a Walton, Hersham and Oatlands Public Utility Company had been formed, underwritten by the Walton U.D.C., which purchased land on both sides of Molesey Road and by March 1927 had started building 32 houses at a price of £575 each. When the company then found itself in difficulties, the Council bought it out and the houses became Hersham's first Council houses. These are the light-coloured houses in the photograph. In 1937 the Council decided to plant 24 trees on the north-west side of that part of Molesey Road, the cost being estimated at 9s. per tree, including guard.

MOLESEY ROAD c.1912

This view, looking north from the corner of Hersham Road, was published by C.F. Ford of Queen's Road. Molesey Road was known until the 1890s as Broad Lane. It was widened in 1906 with the loss of many hedges and roadside trees. The photograph scarcely suggests that traffic conditions warranted such work, but photographers of this period seem to have chosen quiet times for their outdoor work - perhaps wisely, when it involved setting up a tripod in the middle of the road for a long exposure! Just visible on the right is the present (1996) Thresher's Wine Shop, built in 1905, which was taken over by the International Tea Co. around 1909. William Jelley, whose sign can be seen above the passageway beyond, was in business as a gardener and florist here from about 1908 to at least 1916. A little further along, the two blinds at nos. 114-116 belonged to Mrs. Rosina Hancock, grocer and confectioner, and the People's Butcher. The premises are now occupied by SMATS Food & Wine.

ALBANY ROAD c.1913

Laid out about the 1880s on what had been part of a large common field known as Kymsey, Albany Road had, by 1896, about 45 houses unevenly spaced along both sides, most of the gaps being filled within the next fifteen years. The Duke and Duchess of Albany, after whom the road was named, had married on 27th April, 1882, and the event caused much patriotic excitement in the area, triumphal arches being erected along their route from Windsor to Claremont, in Esher. Miss Connolly, who came to live in Hersham as a child in 1892, later recalled that "To live in Albany Road was a passport of respectability, proclaiming impeccable conduct and lineage." Mr. Ford of Queens Road published this postcard, looking east towards Molesey Road c.1914. There was then a coal yard at the western end of the road, and William Fletcher ran a dairy here which was later taken over by the Co-op. The houses were not numbered until 1930, but the house in the right foreground is now number 26.

UNITED DAIRIES VAN c.1935

This photograph was probably taken not long after Triggs' Dairy was taken over by United Dairies. It shows a December 1934 Ford delivery van, probably a Model AA commercial chassis, driven by Mr. Goddard outside 63 Albany Road, where his future wife's parents, Mr. & Mrs. Fred Tickner, lived. Although United Dairies were using motor vans during the 1930s, they reverted to horse-drawn milk floats for a period after the Second World War, probably because of petrol rationing, although it is also possible that some of their vehicles were requisitioned during the War.

19

HERSHAM LIBRARY 1973

G. Emery, recalling his childhood around 1905, recalls: "The only village library.....was held in a small Church Hall, now a bungalow, at noon on Mondays." In July 1937 it was decided that, if suitable accommodation and volunteers were forthcoming, a branch library would be established at Hersham. The Ratepayers Association was approached; Mrs. Evans and Mrs. Carstairs volunteered their services; and the Vicar agreed to allow the Council the use of the St. Peter's Institute in Faulkner's Road at 2s. 6d. (12½p) per session. It opened in 1938 for one afternoon and one evening per week. Later, it was housed in what had been Mr. Vaux's Boys' Club room in Burhill Road. By the 1950s, the County Council had plans to build a new library and in 1954 Walton U.D.C. tried unsuccessfully to persuade them to include a village hall in the project. It was, however, only in 1962 that a suitable plot became available at Pratts Green and the present Library was finally built.

PRATTS GREEN LOOKING NORTH c.1909

Although officially named Lower Green, this small remnant of Walton Common, part of the Poor's Allotment, was popularly known as Pratt's Green after Joseph Pratt, the village undertaker, and later his son Rupert. He also worked as a carpenter and builder. The name J. Pratt & Sons is just visible on the corner of his premises, featured on the left of the picture. Beyond the building was a small pond. The house in the right background was called The Poplars, occupied in 1916 by Mr. F.H. Christian, and originally had more extensive grounds with a range of outbuildings on the site of the first few shops behind it.

SOUTHDOWN ROAD September 1968

On the night of Saturday/Sunday, 14th/15th September, 1968, a heavy rainstorm began unexpectedly, during which 3.2 inches of rain were recorded at Weylands Sewage Works within 24 hours. It affected the whole catchment area of the Mole and Wey, causing widespread flooding in the area. By 4.30 a.m. on Monday the police had to divert traffic from the A3 along Seven Hills Road, and the first evacuations began by 6.00 a.m., after the Mole burst its banks. The water flowed through the Longmore Estate to Molesey Road and onwards. It started to recede during Monday night and by Tuesday afternoon the R.A.F. could begin drying out some houses in Riverside Road. The first houses were re-occupied on Wednesday morning, but the work of drying out houses was not completed until 18th October. 372 Council houses were affected, as well as other property, and at Weylands the Mole changed its course.

ALBANY BRIDGE c.1909

The name "Elmbridge" derives from an early wooden bridge, possibly on this site, crossing the River Mole, then known as the Amele (Emley). By 1606 there was a plank bridge here, but carts used the adjacent ford until an ornamental vehicle bridge was built in the mid-late 19th century when Queen Victoria passed this way regularly en route between Windsor and Claremont. When the road was widened, it was replaced by the structure shown here, completed in June 1906. The County Council and the Walton and Esher Urban District Councils each paid £1,000 towards the cost. The Duchess of Albany, as lord of the manor, was also to have paid £1,000, but offered to pay for a temporary bridge, and later to cover the deficit when the cost exceeded the estimate, bringing her contribution to almost £1,700. Her generosity is remembered in the present name of the bridge. The modern concrete bridge was built in the 1970s as part of a flood prevention scheme to improve the flow of water.

THE NORDIC CLUB c.1958

Near the white cattle bridge in Esher Road stood Halfway Lodge, the old part of which was said to date to the 17th century. The dining room and lower hall were panelled with oak from St. Giles' Church, Cripplegate. In 1932 the house was converted into a restaurant called the Gay Adventure, and a music and dancing licence was granted in September 1932. As it was unlicensed, the Manageress, Mrs. Lacy-Hulbert, started a country club called the Half-Way Club. In 1937 she successfully applied for an on-licence. The club then had 700-800 members. During the 1950s it was known for a time as The Hour Glass and then as the Nordic Club. The photograph shows the swimming pool built in 1933 to the left of the house. There was also a dance floor and bar in a purpose-built extension. When it closed, the business transferred to East Molesey. The house was left empty and was demolished when the road was rebuilt in the early 1960s and The Leys flats built on the site, but the pool was retained for the use of the new residents.

OLD ESHER ROAD c.1900

The main road between Hersham and Esher was a picturesque route bounded by hedges, fields and, on the stretch shown here, by the River Mole on its south side. It was not, however, by modern standards either a wide road or a straight one and was particularly prone to flooding, which frequently rendered it impassable. By the 1950s the Council considered it essential to improve the road and the solution adopted was to build a new dual carriageway and rebuild Albany Bridge, leaving the old road as a cul-de-sac. Because of the risk of flooding, the affected stretch of road was built on an embankment to raise it above the level of the surrounding land. Work started in 1961 but, because of delays over the rebuilding of the bridge, it was not completed until five years later. A number of old buildings alongside the road were demolished in the process, including the Round Chapel and Rockwood.

RIVER MOLE c.1932

Generations of Hersham children must have fished for "tiddlers" at this spot, safe from the traffic passing on the other side of the fence.

In the background is the cattle bridge, built after the Council acquired Longmore Farm for development in 1921 to provide easy access between the land on either side of the river, which was leased for grazing. Cattle trucks would also stop on the Esher Road to load or unload animals which were driven over the river. The bridge was blown up by the army as a training exercise during the 1960s, after it had been declared unsafe. Nearby was a bus stop, together with a small building from which sweets and cigarettes were sold during the 1950s. The roof of the "Gay Adventure" roadhouse is visible among the trees beyond the bridge. To the right of it is a cedar tree, a reminder of the house's prouder days as a private mansion with its own coach house and stables.

ESHER ROAD c.1912

The narrowness of the old main road is perhaps more obvious in this view looking towards Hersham. It posed little hazard in the days of horse-drawn transport but, by the time this photograph was taken, motor vehicles were already beginning to cause some problems, in terms both of safety and of road maintenance. A triangular speed limit sign is visible at the far end of the riverside fence. Behind it, above the trees, are the chimneys of Mole House, an early 19th-century mansion occupied since about 1900 by Baron Profumo, a local benefactor who made his grounds available for events such as the party for nearly 1,000 local children organised to celebrate George V's coronation in 1911, and provided grounds for the local football and cricket teams. The house was demolished in the early 1960s and Kingfisher Close built on the site, but the entrance lodge survives at the end of Mole Road.

Primrose League Fête at Hersham. THE BEE LINE TO THE TEA TENT.

PRIMROSE LEAGUE FETE, 24th July, 1908

The Primrose League, established in 1883, is a political organisation formed in support of the principles of Conservatism as represented by Benjamin Disraeli, Earl of Beaconsfield, who died in 1881. The anniversary of his death on 19th April was celebrated as Primrose Day. The Hersham branch (or "Habitation"), apparently formed some time between 1886 and 1898, was no. 289. About 1907, however, it merged with the Walton & Oatlands Habitation, no. 260, to create the Hersham, Walton and Oatlands Habitation, of which the membership in May 1909 was made up of 621 from Hersham, 190 from Walton and 185 from Oatlands. The photograph shows the queue for the tea tent at the fête held in the grounds of Mole House, made available by Baron Profumo, in 1908. Mr. Albert Profumo was at the time the group's Hon. Sec., while most of the more prominent inhabitants of the village attended the fête. The event included displays by the local Fire Brigade, political speeches, races, and dancing to music by the Weybridge Band. Several fairground rides also proved popular.

1ST HERSHAM SCOUTS AND CUBS, March 1939

The 1st Hersham Scout Troop was established by Mr. R. Henshaw and registered at Headquarters on 27th October, 1912. In 1932 the first Wolf Cubs were enrolled under Cubmaster Mr. J. Pennefather, soon succeeded by Mr. Jack Crowhurst. In 1933 a seven-roomed wooden hut with galvanised roof was purchased from a site near Croydon. This was dismantled and literally carted to the field next to the Football Club, where it became the Group Headquarters. In 1939 the scouts collected waste paper for the War effort and by December of that year about four tons of paper was stored in the hut, together with various items of equipment. On 26th December, 1939, fire broke out. The Walton Fire Brigade and the Hersham Auxiliary Fire Service attended the blaze, but only one end survived, together with some tents stored there. Pictured outside the hut is Scoutmaster Stan Fisher with:

Back row: John Terry, Arthur Spilker, Ron Chalcraft, Eric Howard, Fred Chalcraft, Mick Cockrean, Bob Fripp, Ron Ollis, Jack Mott, ?, Arnie Hicks, Mrs. Hilda Fisher.

2nd Row: Miss Searle, Norman Batchelor, Raymond Howard, ? Arundel, Barron Terry, John Glashier, Philip Grace, Jimmy Garley.

Standing left of table: Peter Lea. Other Cubs unknown.

HERSHAM UNITED FOOTBALL CLUB 1913-14

The Hersham Football Club was founded before 1896. Their fortunes varied, but in February 1913 a meeting of the Hersham United Football Club at the Barley Mow agreed to amalgamate with the Walton Football Club. The Walton Club, however, decided against the merger the following month. In the 1914-15 season the two clubs attempted to form a joint Saturday side in consequence of the number of players who had entered the forces, but could not raise enough men even for a combined eleven. The merger eventually took place in 1945. The photograph shows the 1913-14 team with the Kingston Wednesday League Cup and Chertsey Mid-Week League Cup:

Back: W. Pollard, W. Denley, S.H. Taylor, J. Linnegar, P. Jenvey, H. Gadd, E.W. Hedley (Hon. Sec.)
Middle: L. Felgate (Hon. Treas.), E. Kirby, A.A. Harman (Captain), Baron A. Profumo (President), C. Stacey (Vice-Captain), H. Harman, J. Stanley (Wed. Sec.)
Front: S. Burningham, N. Harman, Dickie Harman (Mascot), C. Rooke, L.E. Harman.

HERSHAM RANGERS (WEDNESDAY) FOOTBALL CLUB 1930-31

This club was formed in June 1926 to provide football for men who worked in local shops and other establishments which, by law, had to close on Wednesday afternoons. Indeed, club officials Harold Sedgebeer, Arthur Cooper and George Elliott were all businessmen owning shops in Hersham. They played in the Kingston and District Wednesday League and, until disbanded early in the Second World War, shared the Mole House ground with Hersham Football Club. The latter now rented the ground from the Kingston Ecclesiastical Charities, who sold it to the Walton & Weybridge U.D.C. after the War. The photograph shows Hersham Rangers after winning the Sutton Wednesday Hospital Cup in the 1930-31 season. They subsequently became finalists in the Surrey County Mid-Week Cup in 1932-33 and winners of the same in 1933-34. Pictured are:

Back: Charles Spratt, Arthur Gosden, F. Purdee, Arthur Crook, Harold Sedgebeer, L. Eastaff, W. Aylott, Cecil Wilby, Arthur Cooper, R. Wright, R. Dedman, G. Gawn, George Merrett.
Front: Jack Hoare (Hon. Sec.), F. Phipps, F. Barrett (Vice-Capt.), J. Steer (Capt.), E. Woods, A. Preece, C. Steer, George Elliott.

ROCKWOOD c.1900

Next to the Round Chapel on the south side of Esher Road stood this curious circular cottage built, like the chapel, by Mr. Andrew Scott of "Lytheys" around 1840. It was constructed of knotted oak pollards, said to have taken 30 years to collect, at a cost of £600. It has been said that Rockwood was probably occupied by Mr. Scott's gardener, although local directories suggest that Andrew Scott or other members of his family occupied the cottage until at least 1899. In 1935 the Rockwood Kennels appear to have been in operation here and by 1938 it was the Rockwood Tea Gardens, run by Albert Edward Cousins. A local resident recalls an advertisement inviting customers to "Come and have tea In the trunk of a tree". To the regret of many, it was demolished in 1951 to make way for the present garage and the dual carriageway.

THE ROUND CHAPEL, 24th April, 1908

In 1839 the Rev. Austin E. Lord came to Walton to found a Congregational Church, preaching initially in a tent. Attempts to obtain a site in Walton proving unsuccessful, Mr. Andrew Scott of "Lytheys" provided land on the corner of Esher Road. The circular building was opened in 1844. Beside it was the Manse, or Minister's house. The pulpit was described in 1883 as "a splendid piece of gnarled oak" from a pollarded tree in Esher Park. In October 1907 a temporary building, the Brampton Gardens Church, was opened in Green Lane, to cater for residents on the new estate off Queens Road and also because of a dispute resulting in the Rev. Herbert J. Crouch being barricaded out of the building. He became the Pastor of the new church and was superseded at the Round Chapel by the Rev. A. Cozens Walker. When the churches reunited in 1913, the old building was left empty. During the Second World War it was used as a sheet metal factory and later a furniture store. The church and Manse were sold for £8,000 in 1958 and demolished in 1961.

HERSHAM COMMERCIAL SCHOOL c.1910

Set back from the road between Mr. Felgate's shop and the Round Chapel was a building which, for a short time at the beginning of this century, housed the Hersham Commercial School, a private establishment run by Mr. Francis Etherington. This group of men and boys, equipped for their summer sports lessons, was photographed outside and includes, back left: Mr. Rupert Pratt, the undertaker, who lived and worked nearby; Mr. Felgate the saddler, with boater and moustache; standing second from left, "Darkie" Doyle; and, standing on the right, Mr. Vaux or possibly Mr. Etherington.

FELGATE'S SHOP 1904

Leonard Felgate, formerly of Kingston, bought this shop at 1, Esher Road in 1900. Primarily a saddler, harness maker and leather dealer, according to the boards on the front of his shop, he was also an agent for Smithers & Sons, furnishing & warehousing, and ran a booking office here for Pickfords Ltd. London Suburban and Universal Parcel Express. In 1916 he was advertising "Football and Cricket Goods kept in stock. Noted for the famous 'Grasshopper' Footballs. Trunks, portmanteaux, and bags.....English leather a speciality." Mr. Felgate's interest in sport did not end with supplying the equipment and he was Hon. Treasurer of Hersham Football Club for some time. He kept up his business into his seventies, dying in 1940 at the age of 77. At the gate can be seen his two youngest children, May and George. The premises subsequently became a hairdresser's and later housed Hersham Press. It has recently been renovated and is now a mobile 'phone shop.

HERSHAM BY-PASS c.1975

The construction of the Hersham By-pass was first projected in March 1925 when the Council was planning the construction of New Zealand Avenue. In September 1929, negotiations commenced for the purchase of the land required for the new Esher Road (work eventually started in 1961), with which the new by-pass would be linked. By April 1938, plans for the by-pass were sufficiently advanced for the Council to purchase just over 11 acres of land between Thrupps Lane, the Mole and Esher Road to compensate for the loss of a large part of the old Hersham Recreation Ground through which the new road was to pass. The outbreak of the Second World War the following year naturally delayed the project! In 1967, after the new dual-carriageway Esher Road was finally completed, the County Council authorised the purchase of the necessary land for building the by-pass. The difficulties involved, together with a period of national economy, further delayed construction, and the road was eventually opened in 1977.

THE BARLEY MOW 1958

One of Hersham's principal surviving landmarks, the Barley Mow, facing onto the junction of Hersham Road and Esher Road, was always well placed to attract passing trade. Probably originally a pair of 17th- or early 18th-century cottages, it had become an alehouse by the 1790s, when it was kept by Thomas Penny. The executors of Durley Grazebrook, a Chertsey solicitor, sold it in 1869 to Bertram Francis Barton of Hersham Lodge. At that time it consisted of a parlour, bar, ante room, tap room, cellar, two wash houses, pump and copper, five bedrooms and linen closet, stable for six horses, loose box, coach house, wood and coal shed and large garden. Barton sold it with Hersham Lodge to Henry Brooks in 1887. On Brooks' death in 1917 it was bought by the Isleworth Brewery Company, which went into liquidation in 1924. It subsequently passed into the hands of Watney Combe Reid & Co. Ltd.

CORNER OF ESHER ROAD c.1908

This photograph shows a scene which has been dramatically altered by the demands of modern motor traffic. While the Barley Mow, run from c.1890 to c.1910 by David McDermott, and Felgate's saddler's shop (now selling mobile 'phones) survive, the other buildings have gone and the junction is now a busy roundabout serving the modern dual carriageway which passes to the right of the inn. The old cattle drinking trough by the lamp-post on the right was one of several in the area which were provided by the Metropolitan Drinking Fountain and Cattle Trough Association in the late 19th century. In July 1937 the Council authorised its removal to a new position and the laying down of a temporary traffic island.

MOLESEY ROAD LOOKING SOUTH c.1935

The junction of Molesey Road and Esher Road seems, from this photograph, to be a quiet spot but, by 1936, the local Highways Committee was discussing means of improving the traffic conditions here. The present by-pass had, of course, yet to be built and the van advertising Chevrolet trucks with the patriotic exhortation to "Buy British" is in the forecourt of the Barley Mow, run at that time by Mrs. Ellen Elizabeth Dixon. Beyond is F.L. Woods' garage, which has at least five different brands of petrol for sale and, behind the petrol pumps, the entrance to the recreation ground purchased by the Council in 1923, and Hersham Lodge. The hairdresser's shop just visible on the corner of Esher Road belonged to A.E.G. Bishop.

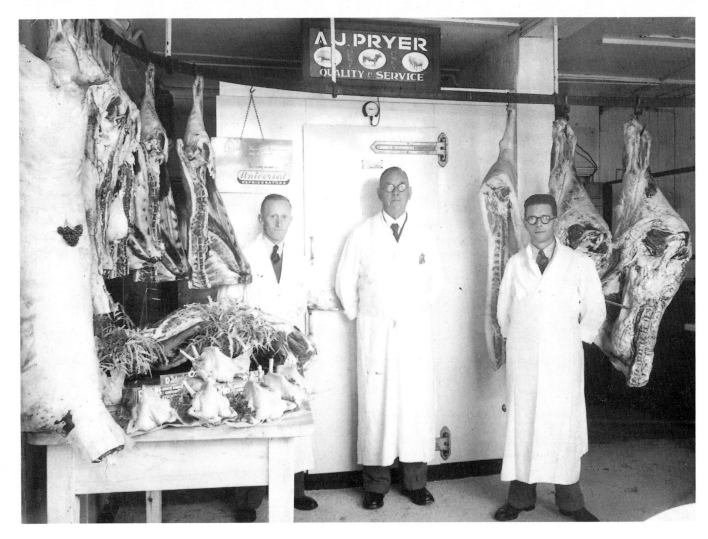

A.J. PRYER'S SHOP c.1935

Albert J. Pryer had been employed by Mr. Grimditch in his butchering business from c.1905, when he came to Hersham, until he took over a butcher's shop at 72 Queen's Road in 1911. Initially, he worked as Manager for the then owner, Ernest H. Smith, at a starting salary of 25s. (£1.25) per week, plus house, fuel, and a commission of 5% on all takings over £25 per week, with a further 10% commission on net profits. His contract included an option to buy a partnership in the business within three years. In 1917, Mr. Pryer purchased Albert James Harman's butcher's shop at 90 Molesey Road, which had been in operation since the 1890s. The exterior view shows a delivery bike, typical of those used by tradesmen in the 1930s who employed boys to make small local deliveries. An earlier photograph of A.J. Harman's shop c.1908 appears to show an old-fashioned open-fronted shop, and the canvas blind above the shop window would then have been an essential protection against the elements for the carcasses which hung in the opening. After the installation of the glass window shown here, its purpose was principally to keep the sun off the meat. The interior view shows the new cold store which had just been installed at a cost of £550. Mr. Pryer is in the centre of the picture and on the right is his eldest son. After more than 35 years here, Mr. Pryer finally sold the shop to Mr. Grimditch in 1954.

ABC MOTORCYCLE 1916

The All British (Engine) Company originated in Redbridge, Southampton, in 1910 and moved to Brooklands in 1912 and, on the outbreak of the First World War in 1914, to a building in Molesey Road opposite Hersham Lodge previously occupied by Faulkner's foundry. The company's design engineer, Granville Bradshaw, began by designing aero engines, but in 1913 the 500cc ABC motorcycle started production, evolving to the form seen here by 1916. For a brief period in 1914 the company's test rider, Jack Emerson, held world records at Brooklands in excess of 80 mph. Production at the Hersham factory soon switched from motorcycles to aero and auxiliary engines for the War effort. The later models were produced only in small numbers for the War Office. This example incorporates leaf spring suspension, which was later used in the post-war 398cc version produced for ABC by Sopwith's in Kingston.

HERSHAM LODGE 1921

On the west side of Molesey Road stood Hersham Lodge, a mansion with seven acres of garden and parkland. It replaced an early 18th-century house on the same site known as Hersham Place and seems to have been built in the mid-19th century. It was bought by Henry Brooks about 1887 and enlarged, making it the largest house in the village. Mr. and Mrs. Brooks lived there until 1917, when they both died. In 1920 ABC Road Motors Ltd. were about to market a new car design, but lacked the capacity to produce it. ABC Motors (1920) Ltd. was formed and became part of the British Motor Trading Corporation, which included the Swift, Bean and Vulcan companies and several motor component manufacturers. Hersham Lodge was purchased from Mr. Brooks' son for use as offices and a new factory was built on part of the grounds behind the house. The photograph shows a Bean car standing outside the main entrance of the house.

HERSHAM

This map is reproduced from the 6 in. Ordnance Survey map of 1934.

ABC FACTORY c.1921

This view of the interior of the new ABC factory behind Hersham Lodge shows a typical engineering works of the period, with machines operated by overhead belt drives. Here, as elsewhere, employees can be seen to have worn collar and tie on the factory floor. Crankshafts are being machined in the foreground. About 1500 ABC cars were produced here before the new factory was sold in 1923 and production was again restricted to the old premises on the other side of the road. Like the ABC motorcycle, they were designed by Granville Bradshaw, but he left the company in 1920 when it was incorporated into the British Motor Trading Corporation. The car used a flat-twin air-cooled engine with the main petrol tank immediately over the engine and filled through the cap of the dummy radiator. It had a unique vertical gate change and was also unusual in having a four-speed gearbox. ABC cars remained in production until about 1927, after which aero and general precision engineering work was undertaken. In 1951 the company was taken over by Vickers Ltd. and closed in 1971.

HACKBRIDGE TRANSFORMER
c.1935

The Hackbridge Company, founded in 1919 at Hackbridge, Surrey, produced electrical transformers and cables. In 1923 transformer production was moved to the former ABC works at Hersham Lodge and became the Hackbridge Electric Construction Company. Transformers are used to transform voltage to the correct value, to multiply electrical phases and to separate D.C. circuits from the A.C. supply system. Cable manufacture continued in the original premises. The photograph, taken inside the works, shows a transformer ready for testing, flanked by two founder Hackbridge employees, Bill Mott and Jim Woodmore, who moved from the old Hackbridge works in 1923. From 1924 the Hewittic Electric Co. Ltd. shared the works. As transformers are nearly always associated with a rectifier, this was an eminently practical arrangement, although it was not until 1947 that the two companies amalgamated as the Hackbridge and Hewittic Electric Co. Ltd.

TRANSFORMER IN TRANSIT
April 1933

Between 1932 and 1940, the Hackbridge Electric Construction Company made four generator transformers for the new Barking "B" power station. After the setting up of the National Grid, it became practical to transmit electricity effectively over longer distances, leading to the building of larger power stations. When it was built, Barking "B" had Britain's largest generators, and the transformers were then the largest in the world at 125,000 h.p. or 93,750 kVA. Each weighed over 100 tons. The second of the four is shown on the Kingston By-pass en route to Barking. The haulage contractor was E.W. Rudd. The 1917 Fowler road locomotive shown in front was scrapped in 1950, but the two Burrell engines, "City of London", built in 1913 (later converted to a showman's engine and renamed "King George VI") and "His Majesty", built in 1920 and shown here at the rear of the load, both survive. The journey was accomplished without mishap, unlike that of the third transformer in March 1936, when the two engines used overturned on the Seven Hills Road.

HACKBRIDGE SPORTS DAY c.1935

The Hackbridge company encouraged social organisations amongst its staff and provided extensive sporting facilities behind the factory for the Hackbridge Sports Association, in which the Company Directors played a prominent part. Football, tennis, bowls, hockey and cricket were catered for, as well as the athletics illustrated here. The annual sports day began in 1926 and included both track and field events, plus more light-hearted contests such as the egg and spoon race. It was followed by a dance in the Works Social Club. A "Surrey Herald" report of June 1936 indicates that the occasion had usually been blessed with fine weather, that year being an exception. Fortunately, the rain held off until the last event, when many spectators were able to shelter in the pavilion. The competitors were unaffected, as the concluding event was "tilting the bucket", during which they could not expect to remain dry! In contrast, the following year's high jump event had to be cancelled because the ground was so hard.

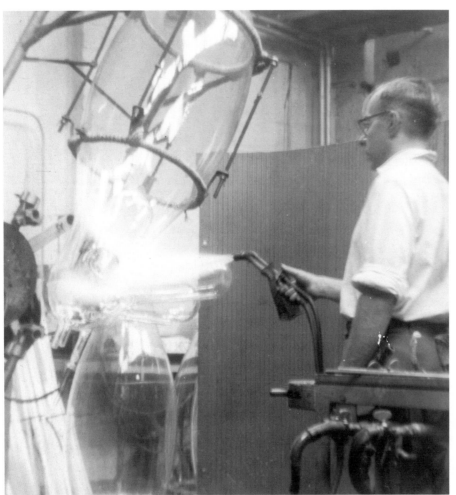

HEWITTIC RECTIFIER PRODUCTION c.1954

The first mercury pool rectifier, developed from the mercury vapour lamp, was produced by Peter Cooper Hewitt in 1904. In 1906 his company, situated beside King's Cross Station, London, was incorporated as Westinghouse Cooper Hewitt Ltd. and in 1920 changed its name to the Hewittic Electric Company Ltd. The early rectifiers were used mainly for battery charging, but as the quality of the glass used was improved, it became possible to produce progressively larger bulbs, extending their possible uses until by 1933 the company could produce equipment able to supply the entire Manchester-Bury line of the London Midland & Scottish Railway. By 1924, the considerable increase in Hewittic's production necessitated expansion of their premises, and they moved to Hersham to share the Hackbridge Electric Co. Ltd. works. The photograph shows Jim Rosewell attaching the anode arms to a rectifier bulb. By this date, the firm claimed to be the world's largest manufacturer of glass bulb mercury arc rectifiers.

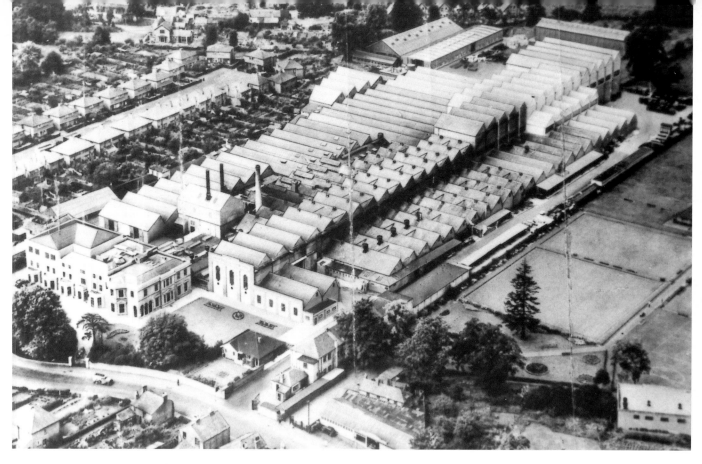

HACKBRIDGE & HEWITTIC FACTORY FROM THE AIR c.1955

The works were extended several times, and between 1925 and 1956 the floor area grew to over four times its original size and the workforce increased tenfold. A former employee remembers that "It was quite a sight in the 1930s when the factory opened and closed each day to see the hundreds of cyclists swarm through the village as the employees went to and from work." In the 1950s the firm joined a group named Combined Electrical Manufacturers, which included switchgear firms, thus enabling complete packages to be offered. In 1967 they merged with English Electric, which was subsequently acquired by the General Electric Company. Rectifier manufacture was transferred to Stafford in late 1971 and transformer production to Stafford and Broadstairs in 1972. The Hersham works closed, and were demolished in 1978. The site is now occupied by the offices and research labs of Air Products Ltd.

CLAREMONT PARADE c.1950

Claremont House was an 18th-century mansion opposite Thrupps Lane and adjacent to Hersham Lodge. In November 1931 the new owner, the Thames Ditton builder A.W. Sheppard, submitted plans to the Council for an estate consisting of 24 semi-detached houses to be built on the site. He was prepared to give the Council a strip of land enabling them to widen the road at this point to 50 feet, on condition that the Council made the necessary sewer connections to a point near the estate entrance. The County Council, however, thought the road widening unnecessary and for the time being would only sanction the construction of a six-foot footpath. In 1933 the old house was demolished and Claremont Close and this parade of shops, called Claremont Parade, were built on the site. Albert E. Ball, grocer, was one of the early occupants of the Parade, at 17 Molesey Road.

HERSHAM HOUSE SCHOOL c.1950

Hersham House, situated on the south side of Thrupps Lane, appears from the Land Tax records to have been built about 1796 by the architect George Shakespear, who is also thought to have built Elm Grove in Walton. He died in March 1797 and the Land Tax records for the following year show the owner of the house as the late George Shakespear and the occupier as Mrs. Jones. Its ratable value was £16. It was enlarged at some time during the period 1870-1896 and in the latter half of the 1890s came into the hands of Arthur Wigram. The Wigram family lived there until at least 1916, but in the 1920s and 1930s it was occupied by Sidney Todd and family. The house was later sold to Mrs. Hewlett, who opened a private day school there for boys aged 3-11 and girls aged 3-18 years. After her death it was sold and demolished c.1984-85 to make way for a housing development.

COMPTON & HERMON'S BODY SHOP c.1922

Compton & Hermon Ltd, coachbuilders, occupied premises behind the present post office and newsagent's in Molesey Road, on the site of Brown's Yard. The car pictured in front of the doors is an ABC chassis of c.1922 with a special thumb-turned aluminium four-seater touring body by Compton & Hermon. Hermon is believed to have ceased any active role in the company after the First World War, and by 1922 the company is listed in a local directory as Compton's Motor Body Builders. The factory later moved to Kingston, and in the mid-1960s to Blagdon Road, New Malden.

GRIMDITCH'S CART c.1905

James E. Grimditch's butcher's shop occupied the northern end of the block which housed Cullen's grocer's shop and post office at the corner of Hersham Green. William James Grimditch took over the business shortly before 1892 from W.H. Mayhead, although James Grimditch had succeeded him by 1905. In the early 1930s he built the slaughterhouse in Berry Lane. The delivery cart shown here was driven by Albert J. (Jim) Pryer, who came to Hersham from Seal, Kent, around 1905 and worked for Mr. Grimditch. In 1909 he married Miss E.F. (Nell) Scott, who became lady's maid to Lady Chitty of Torrie Lodge, Esher. They lived in a cottage in Berry Lane rented from Mr. Grimditch until 1911, when Mr. Pryer became Manager of a butcher's shop at 72 Queen's Road, living above the shop. He later purchased Harman's shop opposite the Barley Mow Inn.

MOLESEY ROAD LOOKING SOUTH c.1925

Seen from near the corner of Thrupps Lane, the most prominent feature in this view is Walter William Wills' outfitter's shop. Mr. Wills, a tailor, arrived in Hersham in 1912 and took over these premises in December 1915. He was advertising himself as "The Ladies' and Gentlemen's Practical Tailor. Ladies' Own Material Made Up" by 1916 when, presumably to stress the up-to-date fashions available, he was careful to point out that he was from London. At that time he would have had competition from the Misses Moores' milliner's shop next door, but at some time between 1921 and the date of this photograph he took over their shop, thus doubling the size of his own flourishing business. Those customers who wished to complete their new outfit with a pair of shoes would only have needed to walk three doors along to 3, Warrington Cottages, just behind the lorry, where J. Jensen had taken over his father's business as a bootmaker in 1905-6. Mr. Wills died in 1945, but his son, Reg, carried on the business until December 1969.

THE WATERMAN'S ARMS c.1910

This photograph was probably taken soon after W.J. Webb took over the Waterman's Arms c.1906. He remained innkeeper here until the mid-1930s. One of Hersham's oldest hostelries, the inn stood strategically in the centre of the village, facing the green and the village pump, which can be seen in the photograph just opposite the door. Inns have always served as meeting places, and from about 1895 to 1907 the Dr. Livingstone Lodge of the Ancient Order of Foresters met at the Waterman's Arms. Earlier, it had been the home of the Hersham Friendly Society, listed in the Quarter Sessions records of 1851. This was one of many such bodies formed during the industrial revolution as a means of mutual assistance for working people before the introduction of the welfare state.

THE WATERMAN'S ARMS c.1950

Structurally little changed, the redecorated Waterman's Arms nevertheless presented a somewhat different appearance by the middle of the 20th century. The Isleworth Brewery Company, which owned it, had perhaps decided to brighten it up in an attempt to attract a "better" class of customer. In 1937 the Council approved a road-widening scheme for the dangerously narrow part of Molesey Road adjacent to the pub, having reached an agreement with the brewers whereby the Company would give the Council a strip of land in exchange for £40 and the rebuilding of the wall in Molesey Road, which was said to be in a collapsed condition. The Surveyor estimated the total cost at £192. The widening would vary from 6 ft. 2 ins to 7 ft. 9 ins., with only 4 ft. 7 ins. off the actual corner. He considered the improvement "the best the Council could possibly get until such time as the Waterman's Arms was demolished...". In the background is Grimditch's butcher's shop.

HERSHAM GREEN FROM THE POND c.1912

This view, produced by C.F. Ford of Queen's Road, shows an interesting group of now-vanished buildings in Queen's Road which were demolished in 1973 to make way for the Old People's Day Centre. The Jolly Waggoners pub, in the centre of the picture, was one of four which faced onto the Green at that date. It was said in 1892 to be chiefly frequented by a "low class of people". Established c.1875, it was run at the time of the photograph by John Sidney Stevens, whose widow, Sarah Ann Stevens, carried on the business until around the beginning of the Second World War. Next door is the old Barclays Bank, which opened c.1906, and to the right of that the Village Hall. Behind the chauffeur-driven car, the local water cart is refilling from a stand-pipe. Watering the roads in hot weather was an essential Council service until tarmacadam solved the problem of dust stirred up by passing vehicles.

THE GREEN c.1903

Hersham Green was originally part of Hersham Common, included in the "Poor's Allotments" under the Enclosure Act of 1800. Although vested in a Trust (now part of the Walton-upon-Thames Charities) for the benefit of the poor of the parish, it came to be regarded as a public open space and used for recreation, for example by the Burwood Cricket Club. After the creation of the Walton Urban District Council in 1895, there was much disagreement regarding the ownership of the various village greens, and Hersham Green, previously maintained by public subscription, fell into disrepair. Strong feelings were aroused, culminating in the creation by the Charity Commission of a new Trust known as "The Poors' Allotments Recreation Grounds" in 1903, enabling the Council to maintain the greens on the rates. Early in 1905, Hersham Green was returfed and a fence erected. Cricket continued, although in 1906 the Council discouraged the recent dangerous practice of playing golf on the Green. The photograph shows the Bank, the Village Hall, Greenside, Astley, Frinton and the Waterman's Arms.

HERSHAM CRICKET CLUB 1911

Mr. Ismel Ewington, who died in 1937 aged 90, remembered the Burwood Cricket Club playing on Hersham Green dressed in black trousers, white shirts, red braces and top hats. On 6th March, 1894, the members of the Burwood and Victoria Cricket Clubs decided to amalgamate the clubs. The disagreement over the ownership of the Green referred to above affected the pitch, but after its restoration an inaugural cricket match was played there on 4th May, 1905, followed by a sumptuous invitation supper. The Council afterwards resolved to purchase a hose for watering the pitch. Annual events included the match between the Hersham C.C. and the tradesmen and a match at Mole House promoted by Baron Profumo and Mr. A. Profumo between the club and their own team. The photograph shows:

Back: J. Waldren (umpire), W. Lawrence, E. Berryman, T. Smith, R. Hamilton, J.E. Dolly, A. Tenniswood.
Middle: J.A. Thompson, W. Colman, H. Alexander, W. Swan (Vice-Captain), W. Poulton (Captain), E. Tickner, A. Smith.
Front: S. Stevens, S. Felgate, H. Trotter (Scorer)

THE VILLAGE HALL c.1950

In the 19th century, in the absence of other evening entertainment, cottagers tended to gather in local inns and alehouses, where they often drank heavily. In the hope of combating this tendency in Hersham, a Village Hall Company was formed in 1884, and in 1886 the building shown here in the right foreground was completed. It was hoped that it would serve as a sort of coffee house and club, and the Trustees hired it out for social occasions. Unfortunately, this was unsuccessful and in 1891 the Trustees instigated the formation of the Hersham Working Men's Club, which leased the Hall. Games facilities were provided and the Club premises became a popular venue for meetings, dances, bazaars, etc. The annual report of the Committee in February 1936 announced an overall profit of £349 16s. 9d., receipts on the bar account totalling £1,476 11s. 2d. When the Village Hall Company went into liquidation in 1946, the Working Men's Club bought the building and continued there until it was disbanded c.1969. The building was demolished in 1973.

NORTH ROAD LOOKING NORTH June 1900

In 1895, Hersham had no gas lighting (first installed in 1896), no piped sewers and most of the village's drains were open ditches. Originally known as Mills's Road North, this narrow, unlit street without pavements and with a central drainage gully was home to some of the poorest inhabitants of Hersham. In 1920, a local chimney sweep with nine children was rehoused here in a cottage with four rooms and a scullery. On Monday, 21st August, 1944, a V1 flying bomb landed at the end of the road, causing considerable damage here and in Primrose Road and breaking windows over a wide area. A row of houses and three allotments were completely destroyed and 38 people injured. The Home Guard, Civil Defence and the Scouts were quickly on the scene to rescue those trapped, and the Congregational Church Hall (which had itself had its windows blown out) and Women's Institute were both put to use as Rest Centres for those affected, remaining open until the Friday.

HERSHAM FROM THE WEST, 25th March, 1972

The scar caused by preliminary clearance work marks the future line of the Hersham By-pass, cutting through the recreation ground to the left of the Hackbridge & Hewittic works in this view by Aerofilms. The junction with Robinsway lies in the bottom left corner of the picture and around it are some of the houses built alongside the intended route between the planning of the by-pass in the 1930s and its eventual construction. Beyond it the new Esher Road is a prominent feature, while the bends of the old road can just be seen amongst the trees and buildings to its right. Snellings Road, North Road and Primrose Road occupy the foreground to the right.

THE BRICKLAYER'S ARMS
c.1909

This hostelry, on the corner of Mills Road, was apparently established around 1865 and William Turner, shown here, took over the licence c.1900-1904. In March 1909, Supt. Coleman opposed the renewal of the pub's licence on the grounds of the proximity of two other fully licensed premises, two beerhouses, two off-licences and the Working Men's Club. (The Red Deer, a beerhouse further along Mills Road, had been de-licensed in 1905 under the Licensing Act of 1904.) The building was situated in a narrow road and had no public urinal, while the other houses had "a good draw up to each, and no obstruction". On the other hand, both the Oddfellows and the Buffaloes met at the Bricklayer's Arms and Mr. Turner considered his trade "the best in Hersham". The licence was granted on condition that the owners, Brandon's Putney Brewery, rebuilt the premises, setting the house back from the road. This photograph was probably taken soon after the new building's completion and the date 1909 can be seen on the cornice. Mr. Turner died on 29th July, 1915.

THE CYCLISTS' REST c.1938

From about 1936, Mrs. Hilda May Sparks ran refreshment rooms known as The Cyclists' Rest in a building rented from Mr. Grimditch at 28 Queen's Road. It appears to have been a typical 1930s tearoom and, as the sign painted on the gable indicates, served teas, home-made cakes, snacks and soft drinks. Mrs. Sparks' political opinions are not known, but she was evidently prepared to allow the premises to be used by those with radical views, as in May 1937 an advertisement appeared in the "Surrey Herald" announcing that there was to be a Blackshirt meeting at the Cyclists' Rest on Wednesday, May 19th. Tickets would be obtainable for 6d or 1s. (2½p or 5p) from Blackshirts selling papers outside the Waterman's Arms that night (Friday) and the following night. Whether any of the local people responded to the invitation is not known